Irish Beauty Doilies™

General Information

Many of the products used in this pattern book can be purchased from local craft, fabric and variety stores, or from the Annie's Attic Needlecraft Catalog (see Customer Service information on page 32).

Contents

Sea Breeze

SKILL LEVEL

INTERMEDIATE

FINISHED SIZE
16 inches square

MATERIALS
- Size 10 crochet cotton:
  225 yds bridal blue
  125 yds each wedgewood blue and
  royal blue
- Size 7/1.65mm steel crochet hook or size
  needed to obtain gauge
- Tapestry needle

GAUGE
Each Motif = 2¼ inches across

PATTERN NOTES
Join with a slip stitch unless otherwise stated.
Chain-3 at beginning of rounds counts as first
  double crochet unless otherwise stated.
Chain-5 at beginning of rounds counts as first
  double crochet and chain-2 space unless otherwise stated.

SPECIAL STITCHES
Chain-4 picot (ch-4 picot): Ch 4, sl st in top of last
  st made.
Chain-3 picot (ch-3 picot): Ch 3, sl st in top of last
  st made.
Joined picot: Ch 2, sl st in designated picot on
  other Motif, ch 2, sl st in top of last st made on
  this Motif.
Triple picot: (Ch 4, sl st, ch 5, sl st, ch 4, sl st) in
  front lp (see Stitch Guide) of last st made.
Beginning cluster (beg cl): Ch 2, *yo twice, insert
  hook in same place, yo, pull lp through, [yo,
  pull through 2 lps on hook] twice, rep from *,
  yo, pull through all 3 lps on hook.
Cluster (cl): Yo twice, insert hook in designated
  place, yo, pull lp through, [yo, pull through
  2 lps on hook] twice, *yo twice, insert hook
  in same place, yo, pull lp through, [yo, pull

through 2 lps on hook] twice, rep from *, yo,
pull through all 4 lps on hook.

INSTRUCTIONS
FIRST MOTIF
Rnd 1: With bridal blue, ch 5, **join** (see Pattern
Notes) in beg ch to form ring, **ch 5** (see Pattern
Notes), dc in ring, [ch 3, dc in ring] 6 times, ch
1, join with dc in 3rd ch of beg ch-5 (counts as
ch sp). (8 dc, 8 ch sps)

Rnd 2: Ch 8 (counts as first dc and ch-5 sp), [dc
in next ch sp, ch 5] around, join in 3rd ch of
beg ch-8.

Rnd 3: Sl st in first ch sp, (**beg cl** —see Special
Stitches, **ch-4 picot**—see Special Stitches, {ch 3,
cl—see Special Stitches, ch-4 picot} twice) in same
sp, ch 4, sc in next ch sp, ch 4, *(cl, ch-4 picot, {ch
3, cl, ch-4 picot} twice) in next ch sp, ch 4, sc in
next ch sp, ch 4, rep from * around, join in beg cl.
Fasten off. (12 cls, 8 ch-3 sps, 8 ch-4 sps)

1-SIDE JOINED MOTIF
Rnds 1 & 2: Rep rnds 1 and 2 of First Motif.

Rnd 3: Sl st in first ch sp, (beg cl, ch-4 picot, ch
3, cl, ch-4 picot, ch 3, cl) in same sp, working
on side of other Motif, **joined picot** (see Special
Stitches) in corresponding picot on other Motif,
ch 4, sc in next ch sp, ch 4, (cl, joined picot in
next picot on other Motif, {ch 3, cl, ch-4 picot}
twice) in next ch sp, ch 4, sc in next ch sp, ch 4,
*(cl, ch-4 picot, {ch 3, cl, ch-4 picot} twice) in
next ch sp, ch 4, sc in next ch sp, ch 4, rep from
*, join in beg cl. Fasten off.

2-SIDE JOINED MOTIF
Rnds 1 & 2: Rep rnds 1 and 2 of First Motif.

Rnd 3: Sl st in first ch sp, (beg cl, ch-4 picot, ch
3, cl, ch-4 picot, ch 3, cl) in same sp, working
on bottom of other Motif, joined picot in corresponding picot on other Motif, ch 4, sc in next

ch sp, ch 4, (cl, joined picot to next picot of other Motif, ch 3, cl, ch-4 picot, ch 3, cl) in next ch sp, joining to side of next Motif, joined picot in corresponding picot on other Motif, ch 4, sc in next ch sp, ch 4, (cl, joined picot to next picot on other Motif, {ch 3, cl, ch-4 picot} twice) in next ch sp, ch 4, sc in next ch sp, ch 4, (cl, ch-4 picot, {ch 3, cl, ch-4 picot} twice) in next ch sp, ch 4, sc in next ch sp, ch 4, join in beg cl. Fasten off.

Work and join Motifs according to Joining Diagram.

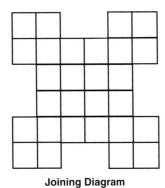

Joining Diagram

EDGING

Rnd 1: Join wedgewood blue with sc in picot before corner picot on top right-hand corner Motif, ch 14, sk next picot, sc in next picot, ch 7, sc in next picot, ch 10, sk next 2 picots, sc in next picot, ch 7, sc in next picot, ch 14, sk next picot, sc in next picot, ch 7, sc in next picot, ch 8, sk next 3 picot, sc in next picot, ch 7, sc in next picot, ch 10, sk next 2 picot, sc in next picot, ch 7, sc in next picot, ch 8, sk next 3 picot, sc in next picot, ch 7, sc in next picot, ch 14, sk next picot, sc in next picot, ch 7, sc in next picot, ch 10, sk next 2 picot, sc next picot, ch 7**, sc in next picot, rep from * around, ending last rep at **, join in beg sc. Fasten off. *(64 sc, 32 ch-7 sps, 12 ch-14 sps, 12 ch-10 sps, 8 ch-8 sps)*

Rnd 2: Join wedgewood blue in first ch-14 sp, beg cl, *(ch 4, cl) 4 times in same sp, ch 5, sc in next ch-7 sp, ch 5, (cl, {ch 4, cl} twice) in next ch-10 sp, ch 5, sc in next ch-7 sp, ch 5, (cl, {ch 3, cl} 4 times) in next ch-14 sp, ch 5, sc in next ch-7 sp, ch 3, (cl, ch 4, cl) in next ch-8 sp, ch 3, sc in next ch-7 sp, ch 5, (cl, {ch 4, cl} twice) in next ch-10 sp, ch 5, sc in next ch-7 sp, ch 3, (cl, ch 4, cl) in next ch-8 sp, ch 3, sc in next ch-7 sp, ch 5, (cl, {ch 4, cl} 4 times) in next ch-14 sp, ch 5, sc in next ch-7 sp, ch 5, (cl, {ch 4, cl} twice) in next ch-10 sp, ch 5, sc in next ch-7 sp, ch 5**, cl in next ch-14 sp, rep from * around, ending last rep at **, join in beg cl. Fasten off. *(112 cls)*

*Note: All picots in rnd 3 are **ch-3 picots** (see Special Stitches).*

Rnd 3: Join royal blue with sc in center cl of first 5-cl group in corner, ***triple picot** (see Special Stitches), sc in same cl, [6 sc in next ch-4 sp, sc in next cl, **ch-3 picot** (see Special Stitches)] twice, (3 sc, ch 3, 3 sc) in each of next 2 ch-5 sps, sc in next cl, ch-3 picot, 6 sc in next ch-4 sp, (sc, triple picot, sc) in next cl, 6 sc in next ch-4 sp, sc in next cl, ch-3 picot, (3 sc, ch 3, 3 sc) in each of next 2 ch-sps, [sc in next cl, ch-3 picot, 6 sc in next ch-4 sp] twice, (sc, triple picot, sc) in next cl, [6 sc in next ch sp, sc in next cl, ch-3 picot] twice, (3 sc, ch 3, 3 sc) in next ch-5 sp, 3 sc in next ch-3 sp, (3 sc, triple picot, 2 sc) in next ch-4 sp, 3 sc in next ch-3 sp, (3 sc, ch 3, 3 sc) in next ch-5 sp, sc in next cl, ch-3 picot, 6 sc in next ch-4 sp, (sc, triple picot, sc) in next cl, 6 sc in next ch-4 sp, sc in next cl, ch-3 picot, (3 sc, ch 3, 3 sc) in next ch-5 sp, 3 sc in next ch-3 sp, (3 sc, triple picot, 2 sc) in next ch-4 sp, 3 sc in next ch-3 sp, (3 sc, ch 3, 3 sc) in next ch-5 sp, [sc in next cl, ch-3 picot, 6 sc in next ch-4 sp] twice, (sc, triple picot, sc) in next cl, [6 sc in next ch-4 sp, sc in next cl, ch-3 picot] twice, (3 sc, ch 3, 3 sc) in each of next 2 ch-5 sps, sc in next cl, ch-3 picot, 6 sc in next ch-4 sp, (sc, triple picot, sc) in next cl, 6 sc in next ch-4 sp, sc in next cl, ch-3 picot, (3 sc, ch 3, 3 sc) in each of next 2 ch-sps, [sc in next cl, ch-3 picot, 6 sc in next ch-4 sp] twice**, sc in next corner cl, rep from * around, ending last rep at **, join in beg sc. Fasten off.

LARGE ROSE
MAKE 5.

Rnd 1: With royal blue, ch 6, join in beg ch to form ring, ch 1, 24 sc in ring, join in beg sc. *(24 sc)*

Rnd 2: Ch 1, sc in first st, ch 3, sk next 2 sts, [sc in next st, ch 3, sk next 2 sts] around, join in beg sc. *(8 ch sps)*

Rnd 3: For **petals**, ch 1, (sc, 5 dc, sc) in each ch sp around, join in beg sc. *(8 petals)*

Rnd 4: Working behind petals, ch 1, **fpsc** *(see Stitch Guide)* around post of first sc on rnd 2, ch 4, [fpsc around next sc on ring 2, ch 4] around, join in beg sc. *(8 ch sps)*

Rnd 5: For **petals**, ch 1, (sc, 7 dc, sc) in each ch sp around, join in beg sc. *(8 petals)*

Rnd 6: Working behind petals, ch 1, fpsc around post of first sc on rnd 4, ch 5, [fpsc around next sc on rnd 4, ch 5] around, join in beg sc. *(8 ch sps)*

Rnd 7: For **petals**, ch 1, (sc, 9 dc, sc) in each ch sp around, join in beg sc. Fasten off.

Sew 1 Large Rose to center of Doily and 1 to center of each 4 corner Motifs.

FIRST SMALL ROSE

Rnd 1: With wedgewood blue, ch 6, join in beg ch to form ring, ch 1, 18 sc in ring, join in beg sc. *(18 sc)*

Rnd 2: Ch 1, sc in first st, ch 3, sk next 2 sts, [sc in next st, ch 3, sk next 2 sts] around, join in beg sc. *(6 sc, 6 ch sps)*

Rnd 3: For **petals**, ch 1, (sc, 5 dc, sc) in each ch sp around, join in beg sc. *(6 petals)*

Rnd 4: Working behind petals, ch 1, fpsc around post of first sc on rnd 2, ch 4, [fpsc around next sc on rnd 2, ch 4] around, join in beg sc. *(6 ch sps)*

Rnd 5: For **petals**, ch 1, (sc, 7 dc, sc) in each ch sp around, join in beg sc. *(6 petals)*

Rnd 6: Working behind petals, ch 1, fpsc around post of first sc on rnd 4, ch 5, [fpsc around next sc on rnd 4, ch 5] around, join in beg sc. *(6 ch sps)*

Rnd 7: For **petals**, ch 1, (sc, 9 dc, sc) in each of first 3 ch sps, working in indentation between corner Motifs on Doily *(see photo)*, (sc, 5 dc, sl st in 2nd picot before inside corner triple picot on Doily, 4 dc, sc) in next ch sp, (sc, 5 dc, sl st in center picot of next tr picot on Doily, 4 dc, sc) in next ch sp, (sc, 5 dc, sl st in next picot on Doily, 4 dc, sc) in last ch sp, join in beg sc. Fasten off.

2ND SMALL ROSE

Rnds 1–6: Rep rnds 1–6 of First Small Rose.

Rnd 7: For **petals**, ch 1, (sc, 9 dc, sc) in each of first 2 ch sps, (sc, 5 dc, sl st in center st of first petal on last Small Rose, 4 dc, sc) in next ch sp, (sc, 5 dc, sk next triple picot on Doily, sl st in next picot, 4 dc, sc) in next ch sp, (sc, 5 dc, sl st in center picot of next triple picot on Doily, 4 dc, sc) in next ch sp, (sc, 5 dc, sl st in next picot on doily, 4 dc, sc) in next ch sp, join in beg sc. Fasten off.

3RD SMALL ROSE

Rnds 1–6: With royal blue, rep rnds 1–6 of First Small Rose.

Rnd 7: For **petals**, ch 1, (sc, 9 dc, sc) in each of first 4 ch sps, (sc, 5 dc, sl st in center st of 2nd petal on First Small Rose, 4 dc, sc) in next ch sp, (sc, 5 dc, sl st in center st of 2nd petal on 2nd Small Rose, 4 dc, sc) in next ch sp, join in beg sc. Fasten off.

Rep First, 2nd and 3rd Roses in rem 3 indentations around Doily. ■

Heart Felt

SKILL LEVEL

■■■☐
INTERMEDIATE

FINISHED SIZE
12 x 13½ inches

MATERIALS
- Size 10 crochet cotton:
  175 yds white
  100 yds burgundy
- Size 7/1.65mm steel crochet hook or size needed to obtain gauge
- Tapestry needle
- 5 x 16mm deep burgundy dagger beads: 6

GAUGE
Rnds 1 and 2 = 1⅜ inches across

PATTERN NOTES
Join with a slip stitch unless otherwise stated.

Chain-3 at beginning of rounds counts as first double crochet unless otherwise stated.

Chain-5 at beginning rounds counts as first double crochet and chain-2 space.

SPECIAL STITCHES
Extended double crochet (extended dc): Yo, insert hook in next st, yo, pull lp through, yo, pull through 1 lp on hook, [yo, pull through 2 lps on hook] twice.

Treble cluster (tr cl): Yo twice, insert hook in designated place, yo, pull lp through, [yo, pull through 2 lps on hook] twice, *yo twice, insert hook in same place, yo, pull lp through, [yo, pull through 2 lps on hook] twice, rep from *, yo, pull through all 4 lps on hook.

Beginning treble cluster (beg tr cl): Ch 2, *yo twice, insert hook in same place, yo, pull lp through, [yo, pull through 2 lps on hook] twice, rep from *, yo, pull through all 3 lps on hook.

Double crochet decrease (dc dec): Yo, insert hook in next st, yo, pull lp through, yo, pull through 2 lps on hook, yo, insert hook around post of next st, yo, pull lp through, yo, pull through 2 lps on hook, yo, insert hook in next st, yo, pull lp through, yo, pull through 2 lps on hook, yo, pull through all 4 lps on hook.

3-double crochet cluster (3-dc cl): Yo, insert hook in designated place, yo, pull lp through, yo, pull through 2 lps on hook, [yo, insert hook in same place, yo, pull lp through, yo, pull through 2 lps on hook] twice, yo, pull through all 4 lps on hook.

4-double crochet cluster (4-dc cl): Yo, insert hook in designated place, yo, pull lp through, yo, pull through 2 lps on hook, [yo, insert hook in same place, yo, pull lp through, yo, pull through 2 lps on hook] 3 times, yo, pull through all 5 lps on hook.

Shell: (2 dc, ch 3, 2 dc) in designated place.

Picot: Ch 3, sl st in top of last st made.

Large scallop (lg scallop): 10 sc in next ch sp, **turn**, ch 2, sk first 2 sc, (dc, ch 2, dc) in next st, ch 2, sk next 2 sts, sc in next st, sl st in next st, **turn**, ch 1, (2 sc, ch 3, 2 sc) in next ch-2 sp, (3 sc, picot, 2 sc) in next ch sp, (2 sc, ch 3, 2 sc) in next ch sp, 3 sc in same ch sp on last rnd as first 10 sc.

Medium scallop (med scallop): 10 sc in next ch sp, **turn**, ch 5, sk first 6 sts, sc next st, sl st in next st, **turn**, ch 1, (2 sc, ch 3, 3 sc, picot, 2 sc, ch 3, 2 sc) in next ch-5 sp, 3 sc in same ch sp on last rnd as first 10 sc.

Small scallop (sm scallop): 8 sc in next ch sp, **turn**, ch 4, sk first 4 sts, sc in next st, sl st in next st, **turn**, ch 1, (2 sc, [ch 2, 2 sc] twice) in next ch sp, 2 sc in same ch sp on last rnd as first 8 sc.

Point scallop: 2 sc in next ch-7 sp, picot, 5 sc in same sp, **turn**, ch 5, sk first sc, sc in next st, sl st in next st, **turn**, ch 1, (2 sc, ch 3, 3 sc, **triple picot**—*see Special Stitches*, 2 sc, picot, 2 sc) in next ch-5 sp, (2 sc, picot, 2 sc) in same ch-7 sp on last rnd.

Triple picot: (Ch 4, sl st, ch 5, sl st, ch 4, sl st) in **front lp** (*see Stitch Guide*) of last st made

INSTRUCTIONS
DOILY
Rnd 1: With white, ch 5, **join** (*see Pattern Notes*) in beg ch to form ring, **ch 3** (*see Pattern Notes*), dc in

ring, [ch 2, 2 dc in ring] 7 times, join with dc in 3rd ch of beg ch-3 *(counts as ch sp)*. *(16 dc, 8 ch sps)*

Rnd 2: Sl st in first ch sp, ch 8 *(counts as first dc and ch-5 sp)*, dc in next ch sp, (ch 5, dc in next ch sp) around, ch 2, join with **extended dc** *(see Special Stitches)* in 3rd ch of beg ch-8 *(counts as ch sp)*. *(8 dc, 8 ch sps)*

Rnd 3: Ch 1, sc in first ch sp, ch 3, (**tr cl**—*see Special Stitches*, ch 4, 3 tr, ch 4, 3-tr cl) in next ch sp, [ch 3, sc in next ch sp, ch 3, (3-tr cl, ch 4, 3 tr, ch 4, 3-tr cl) in next ch sp] around, ch 1, join with dc in beg sc *(counts as ch sp)*. *(12 dc, 8 tr cls, 8 ch-4 sps, 8 ch-3 sps)*

Rnd 4: Ch 1, sc in first ch sp, *ch 5, 2 sc in next ch-3 sp, 4 sc in next ch-4 sp, sc in each of next 3 tr, 4 sc in next ch-4 sp**, 2 sc in next ch-3 sp rep from * around, ending last rep at **, sc in same ch sp as first sc, join in beg sc. *(60 sc)*

Rnd 5: Sl st in next ch-5 sp, **beg tr cl** *(see Special Stitches)*, (ch 4, 3-tr cl) twice in same sp, *ch 3, sk next 2 sc, sc in next sc, ch 4, sk next 3 sc, dc in next st, **fptr** *(see Stitch Guide)* around center tr of corresponding 3-tr group on rnd before last, sk sc behind post st, dc in next st, ch 4, sk next 3 sts, sc in next st, ch 3**, (3-tr cl, {ch 4, 3-tr cl} twice) in next ch-5 sp, rep from * around, ending last rep at **, join in top of beg cl. *(12 tr cls, 8 dc, 8 sc, 4 fptr, 4 sc)*

Rnd 6: Sl st in next ch sp, **ch 5** *(see Pattern Notes)*, dc in same sp, *ch 5, (dc, ch 2, dc) in next ch sp, [ch 3, dc in next ch sp] twice, ch 2, **dc dec** *(see Special Stitches)*, ch 2, dc in next ch sp, ch 3, dc in next ch sp, ch 3**, (dc, ch 2, dc) in next ch sp, rep from * around, ending last rep at **, join in 3rd ch of beg ch-5. *(32 dc, 4 dc decs)*

Rnd 7: Sl st in next ch-2 sp, ch 5, *(**3-dc cl**—*see Special Stitches*, ch 5, 3-dc cl) in next ch sp, [ch 2, dc in next ch sp] twice, ch 3, sc in next ch sp, ch 3, dc in next dc, ch 5, sk next dec, dc in next dc, ch 3, sc in next ch sp, ch 3, dc next ch sp, ch 2**, dc in next ch sp, ch 2, rep from * around, ending last rep at **, join in 3rd ch of beg ch-5. *(40 ch sps, 8 dc cls)*

Rnd 8: Ch 5, *dc in next cl, ch 2, (3-dc cl, ch 5, 3-dc cl) in next ch sp, ch 2, dc in next cl, [ch 2, dc in next dc] twice, ch 5, sk next sc, dc in next dc, ch 2, dc in next ch-5 sp, ch 2, dc in next dc, ch 5, sk next sc, dc in next dc, ch 2**, dc in next dc, ch 2, rep from * around, ending last rep at **, join in 3rd ch of beg ch-5. *(44 ch sps, 8 cls)*

Rnd 9: Ch 5, *dc in next dc, ch 2, dc in next cl, ch 2, (3-dc cl, ch 5, 3-dc cl) in next ch sp, ch 2, dc in next cl, [ch 2, dc in next dc] 3 times, ch 2, dc in next ch-5 sp, [ch 2, dc in next dc] 3 times, ch 2, dc in next dc, ch 2**, dc next dc, ch 2, rep from * around, ending last rep at **, join in 3rd ch of beg ch-5. *(14 ch-2 sps on each side between corner ch-5 sps)*

Rnd 10: Ch 3, *2 dc in each ch sp and dc in each st across to next cl, dc in next cl, ch 2, (3-dc cl, ch 5, 3-dc cl) in next ch-5 sp, ch 2, dc in next cl, rep from * 3 times, 2 dc in each ch sp and dc in each st across, join in 3rd ch of beg ch-3. *(43 dc on each side between corner ch sps)*

Rnd 11: Ch 5, sk next 2 sts, dc in next st, [ch 2, sk next 2 sts, dc in next st] twice, ch 2, dc in next cl, ch 2, (3-dc cl, ch 5, 3-dc cl) in next ch-5 sp, ch 2, dc in next cl, ch 2, dc in next dc, *[ch 2, sk next 2 sts, dc in next st] 14 times, ch 2, dc in next cl, ch 2, (3-dc cl, ch 5, 3-dc cl) in next ch-5 sp, ch 2, dc in next cl, ch 2, dc in next dc, rep from * twice, *[ch 2, sk next 2 sts, dc in next st] 10 times, ch 2, join in 3rd ch of beg ch-5. *(18 ch-2 sps on each side between corner ch-5 sps)*

Rnd 12: Ch 1, sc in first st, [2 sc in next ch sp, sc in next dc or cl] across to next ch-5 sp, *7 sc in next ch-5 sp, [sc in next cl or dc, 2 sc in next ch sp] 9 times, (sc, ch 4, sc) in next dc, [2 sc in next ch sp, sc in next dc or cl] 9 times, rep from * twice, 7 sc in next ch-5 sp, 2 sc in each ch-2 sp and sc in each dc or cl around , join in beg sc. Fasten off.

HEART SIDE
Row 1: With WS facing, join white with sc in 6th sc from first ch-4 sp on last rnd of Doily, ch 1, (dtr, {ch 2, dtr} 5 times) in next ch-4 sp, ch 1, sk next 5 sc, sc in next sc, leaving rem sts unworked, turn. *(6 dtr, 2 sc)*

Row 2: [Ch 4, sc in next ch-2 sp] 5 times, ch 4, sc in next sc, sl st in next st on Doily, sc in next st, turn. *(6 ch-4 sps)*

Row 3: Ch 1, (dc, ch 2, dc) in next ch-4 sp, [ch 2, (dc, ch 2, dc) in next ch-4 sp] 5 times, ch 1, sk next 2 sts on Doily, sc in next st, sl st in next st, sc in next st, turn. *(11 ch-2 sps)*

Row 4: Ch 1, **4-dc cl** *(see Special Stitches)* in next ch-2 sp, [ch 3, 4-dc cl in next ch-2 sp] 10 times, ch 1, sk next 2 sts on Doily, sc in next st, sl st in next st, sc in next st, turn. *(11 cls, 10 ch-3 sps)*

Row 5: [Ch 4, dc in next ch-3 sp] 10 times, ch 4, sk next 2 sts on Doily, sc in next st, sl st in next st, sc in next st, turn. *(11 ch-4 sps)*

Row 6: [Ch 2, sc in next ch-4 sp, ch 2, dc in next dc] 10 times, ch 2, sc in next ch-4 sp, ch 2, sk next 2 sts on Doily, sc in next st, sl st in next st, sc in next st, turn. *(22 ch-2 sps, 10 dc)*

Row 7: [Ch 5, dc in next dc] 10 times, ch 5, sk next 2 sts on Doily, sc in next st, sl st in next st, sc in next st, turn. *(11 ch-5 sps)*

Row 8: [Ch 1, **shell** *(see Special Stitches)* in next ch-5 sp] 11 times, ch 1, sk next 2 sts on Doily, sc in next st, sl st in next st, sc in next st, turn. *(11 shells)*

Row 9: Ch 1, shell in ch sp of next shell, [ch 2, shell in ch sp of next shell] 10 times, ch 1, sk next 2 sts on Doily, sc in next st, sl st in next st, sc in next st, turn.

Row 10: Ch 1, (3 dc, ch 3, 3 dc) in next shell, [ch 2, (3 dc, ch 3, 3 dc) in next shell] 10 times, ch 1, sk next 2 sts on Doily, sc in next st. Fasten off.

Rep on other Doily side beg in 6 sc after next ch-4 sp.

EDGING

Rnd 1: With RS facing, join white with sc between 2 Heart Sides, ch 5, sc in next ch-3 sp, ch 8, dc in next ch-3 sp, [ch 8, tr in next ch-3 sp] twice, [ch 8, dc in next ch-3 sp] twice, [ch 8, sc in next ch-3 sp] 5 times, ch 5, sc in 4th sc of next corner 7 sc group on Doily, ch 6, sk next 6 sts, sc in next st, [ch 6, sk next 5 sts, sc in next st] 8 times, ch 6, sk next 6 sts, (sc, ch 7, sc) in next st, ch 6, sk next 6 sts, sc in next st, [ch 6, sk next 5 sts, sc in next st] 8 times, ch 6, sk next 6 sts, sc in next st, ch 5, sc in next ch-3 sp, [ch 8, sc in next ch-3 sp] 4 times, [ch 8, dc in next ch-3 sp] twice, [ch 8, tr in next ch-3 sp] twice, ch 8, dc in next ch-3 sp, ch 8, sc in next ch-3 sp, ch 5, join in beg sc. Fasten off.

Rnd 2: Join burgundy with sc in first st, (4 sc, **picot**—*see Special Stitches*, 4 sc) in next ch sp, **lg scallop** *(see Special Stitches)* in each of next 6 ch sps, **med scallop** *(see Special Stitches)* in each of next 4 ch sps, **sm scallop** *(see Special Stitches)* in each of next 11 ch sps, **point scallop** *(see Special Stitches)*, sm scallop in each of next 11 ch sps, med scallop in each of next 4 ch sps, lg scallop in each of last 6 ch sps, (4 sc, picot, 4 sc) in next ch sp, join in beg sc. Fasten off.

ROSE

Rnd 1: With burgundy, ch 6, join in beg ch to form ring, ch 1, 18 sc in ring, join in beg sc. *(18 sc)*

Rnd 2: Ch 1, sc in first st, ch 3, sk next 2 sts, [sc in next st, ch 3, sk next 2 sts] around, join in beg sc. *(6 sc, 6 ch sps)*

Rnd 3: For **petals**, ch 1, (sc, 3 dc, picot, 2 dc, sc) in each ch sp around, join in beg sc. *(6 petals)*

Rnd 4: Working behind petals, ch 1, fpsc around post of first sc on rnd 2, ch 4, [fpsc around next sc on rnd 2, ch 4] around, join in beg sc. *(6 ch sps)*

Rnd 5: For **petals**, ch 1, (sc, 4 dc, picot, 3 dc, sc) in each ch sp around, join in beg sc. *(6 petals)*

Rnd 6: Working behind petals, ch 1, fpsc around post of first sc on rnd 4, ch 5, [fpsc around next sc on rnd 4, ch 5] around, join in beg sc. *(6 ch sps)*

Rnd 7: For **petals**, ch 1, (sc, 5 dc, picot, 4 dc, sc) in each ch sp around, join in beg sc. Fasten off.

Sew Rose to top of doily between Heart Sides.

BEAD SPRAY

Thread 6 beads onto white crochet cotton, join with sc in st on Doily on 1 side of Rose, ch 2, pull up 1 bead, ch around bead, [ch 1, pull up 1 bead, ch around bead] 5 times, ch 2, sc in st on Doily on opposite side of Rose. Fasten off. ∎

Summer Blush

SKILL LEVEL

EASY

FINISHED SIZE
12 x 14½ inches

MATERIALS
- Size 10 crochet cotton:
  225 yds pink
- Size 7/1.65mm steel crochet hook or size needed to obtain gauge

GAUGE
Rnds 1–6 = 2 inches across

PATTERN NOTES
Join with a slip stitch unless otherwise stated.
Chain-7 at beginning of rounds counts as first double crochet and chain-4 space unless otherwise stated.
Chain-3 at beginning of rounds counts as first double crochet unless otherwise stated.

SPECIAL STITCHES
Beginning treble crochet cluster (beg tr cl): Ch 2, *yo twice, insert hook in same place, yo, pull lp through, [yo, pull through 2 lps on hook] twice, rep from *, yo, pull through all 3 lps on hook.
Treble crochet cluster (tr cl): Yo twice, insert hook in designated place, yo, pull lp through, [yo, pull through 2 lps on hook] twice, *yo twice, insert hook in same place, yo, pull lp through, [yo, pull through 2 lps on hook] twice, rep from *, yo, pull through all 4 lps on hook.
Picot: Ch 5, sl st in top of last st made.
Double crochet cluster (dc cl): Yo, insert hook in designated place, yo, pull lp through, yo, pull through 2 lps on hook, [yo, insert hook in same place, yo, pull lp through, yo, pull through 2 lps on hook twice] twice, yo, pull through all 4 lps on hook.
Shell: (2 dc, ch 2, 2 dc) in designated place.
Triple picot: [Ch 5, sl st in 5th ch from hook] 3 times.

INSTRUCTIONS
DOILY
Rnd 1: Ch 5, **join** (see Pattern Notes) in beg ch to form ring, **ch 7** (see Pattern Notes), [dc in ring, ch 4] 3 times, join in 3rd ch of beg ch-7. (4 dc, 4 ch-4 sps)

Rnd 2: For **petals**, ch 1, (sc, 6 dc, sc) in each ch sp around, join in beg sc. (4 petals)

Rnd 3: Working behind petals, ch 1, **fpsc** (see Stitch Guide) around post of first dc on rnd 1, ch 4, sc in next ch 4 sp of rnd 1 between 3rd and 4th dc of first petal, ch 4, [fpsc around next dc on rnd 1, ch 4, sc in next ch 4 sp on rnd 1 between 3rd and 4th dc of next petal, ch 4] around, join in beg sc. (8 ch sps)

Rnd 4: For **petals**, ch 1, (sc, 7 dc, sc) in each ch sp around, join in beg sc. (8 petals)

Rnd 5: Working behind petals, ch 1, fpsc around post of first sc on rnd 3, ch 5, [fpsc around next sc on rnd 3, ch 5] around, join in beg sc. (8 ch sps)

Rnd 6: For **petals**, ch 1, (sc, 9 dc, sc) in each ch sp around, join in beg sc. (8 petals)

Rnd 7: Ch 7, sc in 5th dc of first petal, ch 4, [tr in first sc on next petal, ch 4, sc in 5th dc of same petal, ch 4] around, join in 3rd ch of beg ch-7. (16 ch sps)

Rnd 8: Ch 1, sc in first st, ch 6, [sc in next tr or sc, ch 6] around, join in beg sc.

Rnd 9: Sl st in next ch sp, **beg tr cl** (see Special Stitches) in same sp, ch 3, **tr cl** (see Special Stitches) in same sp, **picot** (see Special Stitches), ch 3, tr cl in same ch sp, *[ch 4, sc in next ch sp, ch 4, (tr cl, ch 3, tr cl, picot, ch 3, tr cl) in next ch sp] twice, ch 4, sc in next ch sp, ch 4, (**dc cl**—see Special Stitches, ch 3, dc cl) in next ch sp, ch 4, sc in next ch sp, ch 4*, (tr cl, ch 3, tr cl,

picot, ch 3, tr cl) in next ch sp, rep between * once, join in top of beg cl. (18 tr cls, 4 dc cls)

Rnd 10: Sl st in each of next 3 chs, sl st in next st, sl st in next picot, (beg tr cl, ch 4, tr cl) in same sp, *ch 5, sk next ch sp, **tr dec** (see Stitch Guide) in next 2 ch sps, ch 5, sk next ch-3 sp, (tr cl, {ch 4, tr cl} twice) in next picot, ch 5, sk next ch-3 sp, tr dec in next 2 ch sps, ch 5, sk next ch-3 sp, (tr cl, ch 4, tr cl) in next picot, ch 5, sk next ch-3 sp, tr dec in next 2 ch sps, ch 4, (dc cl, ch 4, dc cl) in next ch-3 sp, ch 4, tr dec in next 2 ch sps*, ch 5, sk next ch-3 sp, (tr cl, ch 4, tr cl) in next picot, rep between * once, ch 2, join with tr in top of beg cl (counts as ch sp). (14 tr cls, 4 dc cls)

Rnd 11: Ch 1, sc in first ch sp, [ch 6, sc in next ch sp] around, ch 2, join with tr in beg sc. (26 ch sps)

Rnd 12: Ch 1, sc in first ch sp, [ch 6, sc in next ch sp] twice, *ch 6, (tr cl, ch 4, tr cl) in next ch sp, ch 6, sc in next ch sp, ch 6, (tr cl, {ch 4, tr cl} twice) in next ch sp, ch 6, sc in next ch sp, ch 6, (tr cl, ch 4, tr cl) in next ch sp*, [ch 6, sc in next ch sp] 8 times, rep between * once, [ch 6, sc in next ch sp] 5 times, ch 2, join with tr in beg sc. (14 tr cls)

Rnd 13: Ch 1, sc in first ch sp, [ch 7, sc in next ch sp] 4 times, ch 7, tr dec in next 2 ch sps, [ch 7, sc in next ch sp] twice, ch 7, tr dec in next 2 ch sps, [ch 7, sc in next ch sp] 11 times, ch 7, tr dec in next 2 ch sps, [ch 7, sc in next ch sp] twice, ch 7, tr dec in next 2 ch sps, [ch 7, sc in next ch sp] 6 times, ch 3, join with tr in beg sc. (30 ch sps)

Rnd 14: Ch 1, sc in first ch sp, ch 7, [sc in next ch sp, ch 7] around, join in beg sc.

Rnd 15: Sl st in next ch sp, **ch 3** (see Pattern Notes), 6 dc in same sp, 7 dc in each ch sp around, join in 3rd ch of beg ch-3. (210 dc)

Rnd 16: Sl st in each of next 3 sts, ch 1, sc in same st as last sl st, ch 9, [sc in center st of next 7-dc group, ch 9] around, join in beg sc. (30 ch sps)

Rnd 17: Ch 1, sc in first st, ch 4, (sc, ch 2, sc) in next ch-9 sp, ch 4, [sc in next st, ch 4, (sc, ch 2, sc) in next ch-9 sp, ch 4] around, join in beg sc. (60 ch-4 sps, 30 ch-2 sps)

Rnd 18: Sl st in each of next 4 chs, sl st in next ch-2 sp, ch 5 (counts as first dtr), (dtr, ch 5, 2 dtr) in same sp, (2 dtr, ch 5, 2 dtr) in each ch-2 sp around, join in 5th ch of beg ch-5. (120 dtr, 30 ch-5 sps)

Rnd 19: Ch 3, dc in each st and 5 dc in each ch sp around, join in 3rd ch of beg ch-3. (270 dc)

Rnd 20: Ch 3, dc in next st, *ch 2, sk next 3 sts, **shell** (see Special Stitches) in next st, ch 2, sk next 3 sts**, dc in each of next 2 sts, rep from * around, ending last rep at **, join in 3rd ch of beg ch-3. (30 shells, 30 2-dc groups)

Rnds 21 & 22: Ch 3, dc in next st, [ch 2, sk next ch sp, shell in ch sp of next shell, ch 2, sk next ch sp, dc in each of next 2 sts] twice, [ch 2, sk next ch sp, (3 dc, ch 2, 3 dc) in ch sp of next shell, ch 2, sk next ch sp, dc in each of next 2 sts, ch 2, sk next ch sp, shell in ch sp of next shell, ch 2, sk next ch sp, dc in each of next 2 sts] 5 times, [ch 2, sk next ch sp, shell in ch sp of next shell, ch 2, sk next ch sp, dc in each of next 2 sts] 5 times, [ch 2, sk next ch sp, (3 dc, ch 2, 3 dc) in ch sp of next shell, ch 2, sk next ch sp, dc in each of next 2 sts, ch 2, sk next ch sp, shell in ch sp of next shell, ch 2, sk next ch sp, dc in each of next 2 sts] 5 times, [ch 2, sk next ch sp, shell in ch sp of next shell, ch 2, sk next ch sp, dc in each of next 2 sts] twice, ch 2, sk next ch 2 sp, shell in ch sp of next shell, ch 2, sk next ch sp, join in 3rd ch of beg ch-3. (120 dc, 20 shells)

Rnd 23: Ch 1, sc in sp between first 2 sts, *ch 2, sk next ch sp, (tr cl, {ch 4, tr cl} twice) in next ch sp, ch 2, sk next ch sp, *sc in sp between next 2 sts, rep from * around, ending last rep at **, join in beg sc. (90 cls, 60 ch-2 sps, 60 ch-4 sps, 30 sc)

Rnd 24: Ch 1, [2 sc in next ch-2 sp, (2 sc, ch 3, 2 sc) in next ch-4 sp, (sc, **triple picot**—see Special Stitches, sc) in next cl, (2 sc, ch 3, 2 sc) in next ch-4 sp, 2 sc in next ch-2 sp] around, join in beg sc. Fasten off. ■

Twilight's Touch

SKILL LEVEL

EASY

FINISHED SIZE
18½ inches across

MATERIALS
- Size 10 crochet cotton:
  150 yds each light purple and royal blue
  100 yds light blue
  50 yds white
- Size 7/1.65mm steel crochet hook or size needed to obtain gauge
- Tapestry needle

GAUGE
Rnds 1–4 = 1¾ inches across

PATTERN NOTES
Join with a slip stitch unless otherwise stated.

Chain-3 at beginning of rounds counts as first double crochet unless otherwise stated.

Chain-4 at beginning of rounds counts as first treble crochet unless otherwise stated.

SPECIAL STITCHES
Popcorn (pc): 5 tr in designated place, drop lp from hook, insert hook in first tr of 5-tr group, pull dropped lp through.

Triple picot: Ch 4, sl st in 4th ch from hook, ch 5, sl st in 5th ch from hook, ch 4, sl st in 4th ch from hook.

Double treble decrease (dtr dec): Holding back last lp of each st on hook, dtr in places indicated, yo, pull through all lps on hook.

INSTRUCTIONS
DOILY
Rnd 1: With royal blue, ch 6, **join** (see Pattern Notes) in beg ch to form ring, **ch 3** (see Pattern Notes), 15 dc in ring, join in 3rd ch of beg ch-3. (16 dc)

Rnd 2: Working in **back lps** (see Stitch Guide), ch 1, sc in first st, ch 2, [sc in next st, ch 2] around, join in beg sc. (16 sc, 16 ch sps)

Rnd 3: **Ch 4** (see Pattern Notes), 2 tr in same st, 3 tr in each sc around, join in 4th ch of beg ch-4. (48 tr)

Rnd 4: Ch 1, sc in each of first 2 sts, **dtr dec** (see Special Stitches) in last and 2nd ch-2 sps on rnd 2, [sk next st on this rnd, sc in each of next 5 sts, dtr dec in last worked ch-2 sp and 2nd of next 2 unworked ch-2 sps on rnd 2] 6 times, sk next st on last rnd, sc in each of next 5 sts, dtr dec in last worked ch-2 sp and first worked ch-2 sp on rnd 2, sk next st on last rnd, sc in each of last 4 sts, join in beg sc. Fasten off. (40 sc, 8 dtr)

Rnd 5: Working in back lps, join light blue with sc in any dtr, ch 3, sc in same st, *sc in each of

next 2 sc, (sc, ch 3, sc) in next sc, sc in each of next 2 sts**, (sc, ch 3, sc) in next dtr, rep from * around, ending last rep at **, join in beg sc. Fasten off. *(64 sc, 16 ch sps)*

Rnd 6: Working in back lps, join light purple in 2nd ch-3 sp, ch 3, sc in same sp, sk next st, sc in each of next 2 sts, sk next st, work rem of rnd as follows:

A. Sc in next ch-3 sp, ch 10, sl st in 10th ch from hook to form ring, ch 1, (sc, hdc, 3 dc, ch 5, sl st in top of last dc made, 2 dc, ch 4, sl st in top of last dc made, dc, 2 tr, ch 4, sl st in top of last tr made, tr, dc, ch 4, sl st in top of last dc made, 2 dc, ch 5, sl st in top of last dc made, 3 dc, hdc, sc) in ring, sc around base of ring, sc in same ch sp on last rnd;

B. Sk next st, sc in each of next 2 sts, sk next st, (sc, ch 3, sc) in next ch sp, sk next st, sc in each of next 2 sts, sk next st;

C. Sc in next ch-3 sp, ch 10, sl st in 10th ch from hook to form ring, ch 1, (sc, hdc, 3 dc, ch 2, sc in last ch-5 sp on last ring, ch 2, sl st in top of last dc made, 2 dc, ch 4, sl st in top of last dc made, dc, 2 tr, ch 4, sl st in top of last tr made, tr, dc, ch 4, sl st in top of last dc made, 2 dc, ch 5, sl st in top of last dc made, 3 dc, hdc, sc) in ring, sc around base of ring, sc in same ch sp on last rnd;

D. [Rep B and C alternately] 5 times;

E. Sk next st, sc in each of next 2 sts, sk next st, (sc, ch 3, sc) in next ch sp, sk next st, sc in each of next 2 sts, sk next st;

F. Sc in next ch-3 sp, ch 10, sl st in 10th ch from hook to form ring, ch 1, (sc, hdc, 3 dc, ch 2, sc in last ch-5 sp on last ring, ch 2, sl st in top of last dc made, 2 dc, ch 4, sl st in top of last dc made, dc, 2 tr, ch 4, sl st in top of last tr made, tr, dc, ch 4, sl st in top of last dc made, 2 dc, ch 2, sl st in first ch-5 sp of first ring, ch 2, sl st in top of last dc made, 3 dc, hdc, sc) in ring, sc around base of ring, sc in same ch sp on last rnd, sk next st, sc in each of next 2 sts, sk next st, join in beg sc. Fasten off. *(8 rings)*

Rnd 7: Join royal blue in any joining between rings, ch 8 *(counts as first tr and ch-4 sp)*, *dc in next ch sp, ch 4, hdc in next ch sp, ch 4, dc in next ch sp, ch 4**, tr around next joining, ch 4, rep from * around, ending last rep at **, join in 4th ch of beg ch-8. *(32 ch sps)*

Rnd 8: Ch 1, *(2 sc, 2 hdc) in next ch sp, (3 dc, 2 tr) in next ch sp, 3 tr in next dc, (2 tr, 3 dc) in next ch sp, (2 hdc, 2 sc) in next ch sp, rep from * around, join in beg sc. Fasten off. *(56 tr, 48 dc, 32 sc, 32 hdc)*

Rnd 9: Join light blue in center tr of any 3-tr group, ch 5 *(counts as first dc and ch-2 sp)*, dc in same st, *[ch 2, sk next st, dc in next st] 3 times, ch 2, sk next st, **dc dec** *(see Stitch Guide)* in first and 6th sts of next 6 sts, [ch 2, sk next st, dc in next st] 3 times, ch 2, sk next st**, (dc, ch 2, dc) in next st, rep from * around, ending last rep at **, join in 3rd ch of beg ch-5. *(72 ch sps)*

Rnd 10: Sl st in next ch sp, ch 4, 4 tr in same sp, *3 dc in each of next 2 ch sps, 3 hdc in next ch sp, 2 sc in next ch sp, sc in next dc, 2 sc in next ch sp, 3 hdc in next ch sp, 3 dc in each of next 2 ch sps**, 5 tr in next ch sp, rep from * around, ending last rep at **, join in 4th ch of beg ch-4. Fasten off. *(96 dc, 48 hdc, 40 sc, 40 tr)*

Rnd 11: Working in back lps, join white with sc in center st of any 5-tr group, ch 3, sc in same st, *sc in each of next 6 sts, (sc, ch 3, sc) in next st, sc in each of next 4 sts, sk next 2 sts, (sc, ch 3, sc) in next st, sk next 2 sts, sc in each of next 4 sts, (sc, ch 3, sc) in next st, sc in each of next 6 sts**, (sc, ch 3, sc) in next st, rep from * around, ending last rep at **, join in beg sc. Fasten off. *(224 sc, 32 ch sps)*

Rnd 12: Working in back lps, join light purple with sc in first ch sp, ch 3, sc in same sp, *sk next st, sc in each of next 3 sts, ch 3, sc in each of next 3 sts, (sc, ch 3, sc) in next ch sp, ch 4, **pc** *(see Special Stitches)* in next ch sp, ch 4, (sc, ch 3, sc) in next ch sp, sk next st, sc in each of next 3 sts, ch 3, sc in each of next 3 sts**, (sc, ch 3, sc) in next ch sp, rep from * around, ending last rep at **, join in beg sc. Fasten off. *(40 ch-3 sps, 16 ch-4 sps, 8 pc)*

Rnd 13: Join royal blue with sc in first ch sp, *ch 4, dc in next ch sp, ch 4, tr in next ch sp, ch 4, dtr in next pc, ch 4, tr in next ch sp, ch 4, dc in next ch sp, ch 4**, sc in next ch sp, rep from * around, ending last rep at **, join in beg sc. *(48 ch sps, 48 sts)*

Rnd 14: Ch 1, sc in first st, ch 2, sc in next ch sp, ch 2, [sc in next st, ch 2, sc in next ch sp, ch 2] around, join in beg sc. *(96 ch sps, 96 sc)*

Rnd 15: Ch 4, 2 tr in same st, 2 tr in next st, [3 tr in next st, 2 tr in next st] around, join in 4th ch of beg ch-4. *(240 tr)*

Rnd 16: Ch 1, sc in first st, **dtr dec** *(see Stitch Guide)* in last and 2nd ch-2 sps on rnd 14, [sk next st on this rnd, sc in each of next 4 sts, dtr dec in last worked ch-2 sp and 2nd of next 2 unworked ch-2 sps on rnd 14] 46 times, sk next st on last rnd, sc in each of next 4 sts, dtr dec in last worked ch-2 sp and first worked ch-2 sp on rnd 14, sk next st on last rnd, sc in each of last 3 sts join in beg sc. Fasten off. *(240 sts)*

Rnd 17: Working in back lps, join light blue with sc in any dtr, ch 3, sc in same st, sc in each of next 4 sc, *(sc, ch 3, sc) in next dtr, sc in each of next 4 sc, rep from * around, join in beg sc. Fasten off. *(288 sc, 48 ch sps)*

Rnd 18: Working in back lps, join light purple in ch sp centered above 1 pc on rnd 12, ch 3, sc in same sp, sk next st, sc in each of next 4 sts, sk next st, work rem of rnd as follows:

A. Sc in next ch-3 sp, ch 10, sl st in 10th ch from hook to form ring, ch 1, (sc, hdc, 3 dc, ch 6, sl st in top of last dc made, 2 dc, ch 4, sl st in top of last dc made, dc, 2 tr, ch 4, sl st in top of last tr made, tr, dc, ch 4, sl st in top of last dc made, 2 dc, ch 6, sl st in top of last dc made, 3 dc, hdc, sc) in ring, sc around base of ring, sc in same ch sp on last rnd;

B. Sk next st, sc in each of next 4 sts, sk next st, (sc, ch 3, sc) in next ch sp, sk next st, sc in each of next 4 sts, sk next st;

C. Sc in next ch-3 sp, ch 10, sl st in 10th ch from hook to form ring, ch 1, (sc, hdc, 3 dc, ch 3, sc in last ch-6 sp on last ring, ch 3, sl st in top of last dc made, 2 dc, ch 4, sl st in top of last dc made, dc, 2 tr, ch 4, sl st in top of last tr made, tr, dc, ch 4, sl st in top of last dc made, 2 dc, ch 6, sl st in top of last dc made, 3 dc, hdc, sc) in ring, sc around base of ring, sc in same ch sp on last rnd;

D. [Rep B and C alternately] 21 times;

E. Sk next st, sc in each of next 4 sts, sk next st, (sc, ch 3, sc) in next ch sp, sk next st, sc in each of next 4 sts, sk next st;

F. Sc in next ch-3 sp, ch 10, sl st in 10th ch from hook to form ring, ch 1, (sc, hdc, 3 dc, ch 3, sc in last ch-6 sp on last ring, ch 3, sl st in top of last dc made, 2 dc, ch 4, sl st in top of last dc made, dc, 2 tr, ch 4, sl st in top of last tr made, tr, dc, ch 4, sl st in top of last dc made, 2 dc, ch 3, sl st in first ch-6 sp of first ring, ch 3, sl st in top of last dc made, 3 dc, hdc, sc) in ring, sc around base of ring, sc in same ch sp on last rnd, sk next st, sc in each of next 4 sts, sk next st, join in beg sc. Fasten off. *(24 rings)*

Rnd 19: Join royal blue in any joining between rings, ch 8 *(counts as first tr and ch-4 sp)*, *dc in next ch sp, ch 4, hdc in next ch sp, ch 4, dc in next ch sp, ch 4**, tr around next joining, ch 4, rep from * around, ending last rep at **, join in 4th ch of beg ch-8. *(96 ch sps)*

Rnd 20: Ch 1, *(sc, 2 hdc) in next ch sp, (3 dc, 2 tr) in next ch sp, 3 tr in next dc, (2 tr, 3 dc) in next ch sp, (2 hdc, sc) in next ch sp, rep from * around, join in beg sc. Fasten off. *(168 tr, 144 dc, 96 hdc, 48 sc)*

Rnd 21: Join light blue in 3rd tr of any 3-tr group, ch 5 *(counts as first dc and ch-2 sp)*, dc in same st, *[ch 2, sk next st, dc in next st] 3 times, ch 1, sk next st, dc dec in first and 4th of next 4 sts, ch 1, sk next st, [dc in next st, ch 2, sk next st] 3 times**, (dc, ch 2, dc) in next st, rep from * around, ending last rep at **, join in 3rd ch of beg ch-5. *(216 ch sps)*

Rnd 22: Sl st in next ch sp, ch 4, 4 tr in same sp, *3 dc in each of next 2 ch sps, 2 hdc in next ch sp, sc in each of next 2 ch sps, 2 hdc in next ch sp, 3 dc in each of next 2 ch sps**, 5 tr in next ch sp, rep from * around, ending last rep at **, join in 4th ch of beg ch-4. Fasten off. *(23 sts on each point)*

Rnd 23: Working in back lps, join white with sc in center st of any 5-tr group, ch 3, sc in same st, *[sc in each of next 2 sts, (sc, ch 3, sc) in next st] twice, sc in each of next 3 sts, sk next 4 sts, sc in each of next 3 sts, [(sc, ch 3, sc) in next st, sc in each of next 2 sts] twice**, (sc, ch 3, sc) in next st, rep from * around, ending last rep at **, join in beg sc. Fasten off. *(24 sc, 5 ch sps on each point)*

Rnd 24: Working back lps, join light purple with sc in center ch sp on 1 point, **triple picot** *(see Special Stitches)*, sc in same sp, *[sk next st, sc in each of next 2 sts, (sc, ch 3, sc) in next ch sp] twice, ch 1, (sc, ch 3, sc) in next ch sp on next point, sk next st, sc in each of next 2 sts, (sc, ch 3, sc) in next ch sp, sk next st, sc in each of next 2 sts**, (sc, triple picot, sc) in next ch sp at point, rep from * around, ending last rep at **, join in beg sc. Fasten off.

CENTER ROSE

Rnd 1: With white, ch 6, join in beg ch to form ring, ch 1, 24 sc in ring, join in beg sc. *(24 sc)*

Rnd 2: Ch 1, sc in first st, ch 3, sk next 2 sts, [sc in next st, ch 3, sk next 2 sts] around, join in beg sc. *(8 ch sps)*

Rnd 3: For **petals**, ch 1, (sc, 5 dc, sc) in each ch sp around, join in beg sc. *(8 petals)*

Rnd 4: Working behind petals, ch 1, **fpsc** *(see Stitch Guide)* around post of first sc on rnd 2, ch 4, [fpsc around next sc on ring 2, ch 4] around, join in beg sc. *(8 ch sps)*

Rnd 5: For **petals**, ch 1, (sc, 7 dc, sc) in each ch sp around, join in beg sc. *(8 petals)*

Rnd 6: Working behind petals, ch 1, fpsc around post of first sc on rnd 4, ch 5, [fpsc around next sc on rnd 4, ch 5] around, join in beg sc. *(8 ch sps)*

Rnd 7: For **petals**, ch 1, (sc, 9 dc, sc) in each ch sp around, join in beg sc. Fasten off.

Sew to center of Doily.

OUTER ROSE

Rnd 1: With white, ch 6, join in beg ch to form ring, ch 1, 18 sc in ring, join in beg sc. *(18 sc)*

Rnd 2: Ch 1, sc in first st, ch 3, sk next 2 sts, [sc in next st, ch 3, sk next 2 sts] around, join in beg sc. *(6 sc, 6 ch sps)*

Rnd 3: For **petals**, ch 1, (sc, 5 dc, sc) in each ch sp around, join in beg sc. *(6 petals)*

Rnd 4: Working behind petals, ch 1, **fpsc** *(see Stitch Guide)* around post of first sc on rnd 2, ch 4, [fpsc around next sc on rnd 2, ch 4] around, join in beg sc. *(6 ch sps)*

Rnd 5: For **petals**, ch 1, (sc, 7 dc, sc) in each ch sp around, join in beg sc. *(6 petals)*

Rnd 6: Working behind petals, ch 1, fpsc around post of first sc on rnd 4, ch 5, [fpsc around next sc on rnd 4, ch 5] around, join in beg sc. *(6 ch sps)*

Rnd 7: For **petals**, ch 1, (sc, 9 dc, sc) in each of first 4 ch sps, (sc, 5 dc, sl st in first ch-3 sp after any triple picot on Doily, 4 dc, sc) in next ch sp, (sc, 5 dc, sl st in next ch-3 sp before next triple picot on Doily, 4 dc, sc) in last ch sp, join in beg sc. Fasten off.

Rep Outer Rose between each sp between triple picots around entire outer edge of Doily, ending with 24 Outer Roses. ■

Morning Sunshine

SKILL LEVEL

INTERMEDIATE

FINISHED SIZE

14½ inches across

MATERIALS

- Size 10 crochet cotton:
  350 yds white
- Size 7/1.65mm steel crochet hook or size needed to obtain gauge
- Tapestry needle

GAUGE

Rnds 1 and 2 = 1¼ inches across

PATTERN NOTE

Join with a slip stitch unless otherwise stated.

SPECIAL STITCHES

Popcorn (pc): 6 dc in designated place, drop lp from hook, insert hook in first dc of 6-dc group, pull dropped lp through.

Triple treble crochet (trtr): Yo 4 times, insert hook in designated st, yo, pull lp through, [yo, pull through 2 lps on hook] 5 times.

Triple picot: (Ch 4, sl st, ch 5, sl st, ch 4, sl st) in **front lp** (see Stitch Guide) of last st made.

Beginning cluster (beg cl): Ch 2, [yo, insert hook in same place, yo, pull lp through, yo, pull through 2 lps on hook] twice, yo, pull through all 3 lps on hook.

3-double crochet cluster (3-dc cl): Yo, insert hook in designated place, yo, pull lp through, yo, pull through 2 lps on hook, [yo, insert hook in same place, yo, pull lp through, yo, pull through 2 lps on hook] twice, yo, pull through all 4 lps on hook.

4-double crochet cluster (4-dc cl): Yo, insert hook in designated place, yo, pull lp through, yo, pull through 2 lps on hook, [yo, insert hook in same place, yo, pull lp through, yo, pull through 2 lps on hook] 3 times, yo, pull through all 5 lps on hook.

INSTRUCTIONS
DOILY

Rnd 1: Ch 5, **join** (see Pattern Note) in beg ch to form ring, ch 1, 12 sc in ring, join in beg sc. (12 sc)

Rnd 2: **Beg cl** (see Special Stitches) in first st, ch 3, **3-dc cl** (see Special Stitches) in same st, ch 2, sk next 2 sts, *(3-dc cl, ch 3, 3-dc cl) in next st, ch 2, sk next 2 sts, rep from * around, join in top of beg cl. (8 cls, 4 ch-3 sps, 4 ch-2 sps)

Rnd 3: (Sl st, beg cl, ch 3, 3-dc cl) in first ch-3 sp, ch 3, dc in next ch sp, ch 3, *(3-dc cl, ch 3, 3-dc cl) in next ch sp, ch 3, dc in next ch sp, ch 3, rep from * around, join in top of beg cl. (8 cls, 4 dc)

Rnd 4: (Sl st, beg cl, ch 3, 3-dc cl) in first ch-3 sp, [ch 2, dc in next ch sp] twice, ch 2, *(3-dc cl, ch 3, 3-dc cl) in next ch-3 sp, [ch 2, dc in next ch sp] twice, ch 2, rep from * around, join in top of beg cl. (9 ch-2 sps, 8 cls, 8 dc)

Rnd 5: (Sl st, beg cl, ch 3, 3-dc cl) in first ch-3 sp, *ch 2, dc in next cl, [ch 2, dc in next st] twice, ch 2, dc in next cl, ch 2**, (3-dc cl, ch 3, 3-dc cl) in next ch-3 sp, rep from * around, ending last rep at **, join in top of beg cl. (20 ch-2 sps, 16 dc, 8 cls)

Rnd 6: (Sl st, beg cl, ch 3, 3-dc cl) in first ch-3 sp, *ch 2, dc in next cl, [ch 2, dc in next st] twice, 2 dc in next ch sp, dc in next st, ch 2, dc in next dc, ch 2, dc in next cl, ch 2**, (3-dc cl, ch 3, 3-dc cl) in next ch-3 sp, rep from * around, ending last rep at **, join in top of beg cl. (32 dc, 24 ch-2 sps, 8 cls)

Rnd 7: (Sl st, beg cl, ch 3, 3-dc cl) in first ch-3 sp, *ch 2, dc in next cl, [ch 2, dc in next st] twice, 2 dc in next ch sp, dc in next st, ch 1, **pc** (see Special Stitches) in sp between next 2 dc, ch 1, sk next dc, dc in next dc, 2 dc in next ch sp, dc in next dc, ch 2, dc in next dc, ch 2, dc in next cl, ch 2**, (3-dc cl, ch 3, 3-dc cl) in next ch-3 sp, rep from * around, ending last rep at **, join in top of beg cl. (48 dc, 8 cls, 4 pc)

Rnd 8: (Sl st, beg cl, ch 3, 3-dc cl) in first ch-3 sp, *ch 2, dc in next cl, [ch 2, dc in next st] 3 times, ch 2, sk next 2 dc, dc in next st, dc in next ch-1 sp, sk next pc, dc in next ch-1 sp, dc in next st, ch 2, sk next 2 sts, dc in next st, [ch 2, dc in next st] twice, ch 2, dc in next cl, ch 2**, (3-dc cl, ch 3, 3-dc cl) in next ch-3 sp, rep from * around, ending last rep at **, join in top of beg cl. (48 dc, 8 cls)

Rnd 9: (Sl st, beg cl, ch 3, 3-dc cl) in first ch-3 sp, *ch 2, dc in next cl, [ch 2, dc in next dc] 5 times, ch 2, sk next 2 sts, dc in next st, [ch 2, sc in next dc] 4 times, ch 2, dc in next cl, ch 2**, (3-dc cl, ch 3, 3-dc cl) in next ch-3 sp, rep from * around, ending last rep at **, join in top of beg cl. (52 ch-2 sps, 48 dc, 8 cls)

Rnd 10: (Sl st, beg cl, ch 3, 3-dc cl) in first ch-3 sp, *ch 2, dc in next cl, [2 dc in next ch sp, dc in next dc] 12 times, 2 dc in next ch sp, dc in top of next cl, ch 2**, (3-dc cl, ch 3, 3-dc cl) in next ch-3 sps, rep from * around, ending last rep at **, join in beg cl. (160 dc, 8 cls)

Rnd 11: (Sl st, beg cl, ch 3, 3-dc cl) in first ch-3 sp, *ch 2, dc in next cl, ch 2, dc in next dc, [ch 2, sk next 2 sts, dc in next st] 13 times, ch 2, dc in next cl, ch 2**, (3-dc cl, ch 3, 3-dc cl) in next ch-3 sp, rep from * around, ending last rep at **, join in beg cl. (68 ch-2 sps, 64 dc, 8 cls)

Rnd 12: Sl st in next ch sp, ch 1, 5 sc in same sp, *sc in next cl, [2 sc in next ch sp, sc in next st] 6 times, ch 1, sk next 2 ch sps, (**trtr**—see Special Stitches, {ch 3, trtr} 5 times) in next ch sp, ch 1, sk next 2 ch sps, sc in next dc, [2 sc in next ch sp, sc in next st] 5 times, 2 sc in next ch sp, sc in next cl**, 5 sc in next ch-3 sp, rep from * around, ending last rep at **, join in beg sc. Fasten off. (38 sc, 6 trtr and 2 ch-1 sps on each side between corner 5-sc groups)

SIDE PANEL
Row 1: With WS facing, working on last rnd of Doily, join with sc in 3rd sc from first ch-1 sp on 1 side, ch 1, tr in next ch-1 sp, [ch 2, (tr, ch 2, tr) in next ch-3 sp] 5 times, ch 2, tr in next ch-1 sp, ch 1, sk next 2 sts, sc in next st, sl st in each of next 3 sts, leaving rem sts unworked, turn. (12 tr, 11 ch-2 sps, 2 ch-1 sps)

Row 2: Ch 1, sc in first st, ch 1, 4-**dc cl** (see Special Stitches) in next ch-2 sp, [ch 3, 4-**dc cl** in next ch-2 sp] 10 times, ch 1, sk next 2 sc on Doily, sc in next st, sl st in each of next 3 sts, turn. (11 cls, 10 ch-3 sps)

Row 3: Ch 1, sc in first st, ch 2, dc in next ch-3 sp, [ch 4, dc in next ch-3 sp] 9 times, ch 2, sk next 2 sc on Doily, sc in next st, sl st in each of next 3 sts, turn. (10 dc, 9 ch-4 sps)

Row 4: Ch 1, sc in first st, ch 2, (2 dc, ch 2, 2 dc) in each of next 9 ch-4 sps, ch 2, sk next 2 sts on Doily, sc in next st, sl st in each of next 3 sts, turn. (36 dc, 11 ch-2 sps)

Row 5: Ch 1, sc in first st, ch 2, sk next ch-2 sp, (2 dc, ch 3, 2 dc) in next ch-2 sp, [ch 1, (2 dc, ch 3, 2 dc) in next ch-2 sp] 8 times, ch 2, sk next 2 sts on Doily, sc in next st, sl st in each of next 3 sts, turn. (36 dc, 9 ch-3 sps)

Row 6: Ch 1, sc in first st, ch 2, (3 dc, ch 3, 3 dc) in next ch-3 sp, [ch 1, (3 dc, ch 3, 3 dc) in next ch-3 sp] 8 times, ch 2, sk next 2 sts on Doily, sc in next st. Fasten off.

Rep Side Panel on rem 3 sides of Doily.

CORNER ROSE
Rnd 1: With white, ch 6, join in beg ch to form ring, ch 1, 18 sc in ring, join in beg sc. (18 sc)

Rnd 2: Ch 1, sc in first st, ch 3, sk next 2 sts, [sc in next st, ch 3, sk next 2 sts] around, join in beg sc. (6 sc, 6 ch sps)

Rnd 3: For **petals**, ch 1, (sc, 5 dc, sc) in each ch sp around, join in beg sc. (6 petals)

Rnd 4: Working behind petals, ch 1, **fpsc** (see Stitch Guide) around post of first sc on rnd 2, ch 4, [fpsc around next sc on rnd 2, ch 4] around, join in beg sc. (6 ch sps)

Rnd 5: For **petals**, ch 1, (sc, 4 dc) in first sp, sl st in center sc of 1 corner 5-sc group on Doily, (3 dc, sc) in same ch sp on Rose, (sc, 4 dc) in next ch sp, sl st in next ch-3 sp on Side Panel, (3 dc, sc) in same sp on Rose, (sc, 7 dc, sc) in each of next 3 ch sps, (sc, 4 dc) in last ch sp, sl st in corresponding ch-3 sp on Side Panel, (3 dc, sc) in same ch sp on Rose, join in beg sc. Fasten off.

Row 6: Now working in rows, with WS facing, join with sc in first ch-1 sp on Side Panel after Rose joining, [ch 6, sc in center st of next petal on Rose] 3 times, ch 6, sc in next ch-1 sp after joining on next Side Panel, sl st in each next 3 sts, sl st in next ch-3 sp, turn. *(4 ch-6 sps)*

Row 7: Ch 1, sc in same sp, ch 1, (3 dc, ch 3, 3 dc) in next ch-6 sp, [ch 2, sc in next sc, ch 2, (3 dc, ch 3, 3 dc) in next ch-6 sp] 3 times, ch 1, sc in next ch-3 sp on Side Panel. Fasten off.

Rep on 3 rem corners of Doily.

EDGING
Rnd 1: Join with sc in ch-1 sp on Side Panel before 1 Corner Rose, *ch 7, sc in next ch-3 sp on Corner Rose, [ch 9, sc in next ch-3 sp] 3 times, ch 7, sc in next ch-1 sp on next Side Panel, ch 4, sc in next ch-3 sp, [ch 7, sc in next ch-3 sp] 4 times, ch 4**, sc in next ch-1 sp, rep from * around, ending last rep at **, join in beg sc. *(24 ch-7 sps, 12 ch-9 sps, 8 ch-4 sps)*

Rnd 2: Ch 1, *(4 sc, ch 3, 4 sc) in next ch-7 sp, (4 sc, {ch 3, 4 sc} twice) in next ch-9 sp, 9 sc in next ch-9 sp, **turn**, ch 2, sk next 2 sts, (dc, ch 2, dc) in next sc, ch 2, sk next 2 sc, sc in next sc, **turn**, ch 1, (2 sc, ch 3, 2 sc) in next ch-2 sp, (3 sc, **triple picot**—*see Special Stitches*, 2 sc) in next ch-2 sp, (2 sc, ch 3, 2 sc) in next ch-2 sp, 4 sc in same ch-9 sp on last rnd, (4 sc, {ch 3, 4 sc} twice) in next ch-9 sp, (4 sc, ch 3, 4 sc) in next ch-7 sp, 4 sc in next ch-4 sp, (5 sc, triple picot, 4 sc) in next ch-7 sp, 8 sc in next ch-7 sp, sc in next sc, 4 sc in next ch-7 sp, **turn**, ch 3, sk next 3 sc, (tr, ch 3, tr) in next sc, ch 3, sk next 3 sc, sc in next sc, sl st in next sc, **turn**, ch 1, (3 sc, ch 3, 3 sc) in next ch-2 sp, (4 sc, triple picot, 3 sc) in next ch-3 sp, (3 sc, ch 3, 3 sc) in next ch-3 sp, 4 sc in same ch-7 sp on last rnd, (5 sc, triple picot, 4 sc) in next ch-7 sp, 4 sc in next ch-4 sp, rep rem * around, join in beg sc. Fasten off.

CENTER ROSE
Rnd 1: Ch 6, join in beg ch to form ring, ch 1, 16 sc in ring, join in beg sc. *(16 sc)*

Rnd 2: Ch 1, sc in first st, ch 3, sk next st, [sc in next st, ch 3, sk next st] around, join in beg sc. *(8 ch sps)*

Rnd 3: For **petals**, ch 1, (sc, 5 dc, sc) in each ch sp around, join in beg sc. *(8 petals)*

Rnd 4: Working behind petals, ch 1, **fpsc** *(see Stitch Guide)* around post of first sc on rnd 2, ch 4, [fpsc around next sc on ring 2, ch 4] around, join in beg sc. *(8 ch sps)*

Rnd 5: For **petals**, ch 1, (sc, 7 dc, sc) in each ch sp around, join in beg sc. Fasten off. *(8 petals)*

Sew to center of Doily. ■

Wreath of ROSES

SKILL LEVEL
◼◼◼◻
INTERMEDIATE

FINISHED SIZE
17¾ inches across

MATERIALS
- Size 10 crochet cotton:
  75 yds frosty green
  65 yds light pink
  50 yds ecru
  30 yds each medium pink and burgundy
- Size 7/1.65mm steel crochet hook or size needed to obtain gauge
- Stitch marker

GAUGE
Center Rose = 2½ inches across

PATTERN NOTE
Join with a slip stitch unless otherwise stated.

SPECIAL STITCHES
Beginning cluster (beg cl): Ch 2, *yo twice, insert hook in same place, yo, pull lp through, [yo, pull through 2 lps on hook] twice, rep from *, yo, pull through all 3 lps on hook.
Cluster (cl): Yo twice, insert hook in designated place, yo, pull lp through, [yo, pull through 2 lps on hook] twice, *yo twice, insert hook in same place, yo, pull lp through, [yo, pull through 2 lps on hook] twice, rep from *, yo, pull through all 4 lps on hook.
Picot: Sl st in 4th ch from hook.

INSTRUCTIONS
DOILY
Rnd 1: With light pink, ch 6, **join** (see Pattern Note) in beg ch to form ring, ch 1, 18 sc in ring, join in beg sc. (18 sc)

Rnd 2: Ch 1, sc in first st, ch 3, sk next 2 sts, [sc in next st, ch 3, sk next 2 sts] around, join in beg sc. (6 ch-3 sps)

Rnd 3: For **petals**, ch 1, (sc, 5 dc, sc) in each ch sp around, join in beg sc. (6 petals)

Rnd 4: Working behind petals, ch 1, **fpsc** (see Stitch Guide) around post of first sc on rnd 2, ch 4, [fpsc around next sc on rnd 2, ch 4] around, join in beg sc. (6 ch sps)

Rnd 5: For **petals**, ch 1, (sc, 7 dc, sc) in each ch sp around, join in beg sc. Fasten off. (6 petals)

Rnd 6: Join frosty green in first sc of any petal, ch 7 (counts as first dc and ch-4 sp), sc in center dc of same petal, ch 4, [dc in first sc of next petal, ch 4, sc in center dc of same petal, ch 4] around, join in 3rd ch of beg ch-7. (12 ch sps)

Rnd 7: Ch 1, (sc, 3 dc, sc) in each ch sp around, join in beg sc. Fasten off.

Rnd 8: Join ecru with sc in center st of any 3-dc group, [ch 6, sc center st of next 3-dc group] around, ch 2, join with tr in first sc (counts as ch sp). (12 ch sps)

Rnd 9: Ch 1, sc in first ch sp, *ch 5, **picot** (see Special Stitches), ch 6, picot, ch 2**, sc in next ch sp, rep from * around, ending last rep at **, join in beg sc. (24 picots)

Rnd 10: Sl st across chs to between first 2 picots, ch 1, sc in same sp, [ch 6, picot] twice, ch 3, *sc between next 2 picots, [ch 6, picot] twice, ch 3, rep from * around, join in beg sc.

Rnd 11: Sl st across chs to between first 2 picots, **beg cl** (see Special Stitches) in same ch sp, ch 6, **cl** (see Special Stitches) in same sp, [ch 6, (cl, ch 6, cl) in sp between next 2 picots] around, ch 2, join with tr in top of first cl. (24 cls, 24 ch sps)

Rnd 12: Ch 1, sc in first ch sp, ch 5, picot, ch 6, picot, ch 2, [sc in next ch sp, ch 5, picot, ch 6, picot, ch 2] around, join in beg sc. (48 picot, 24 sc)

Rnd 13: Sl st across chs to between first 2 picots, ch 7 *(counts as first tr and ch-3 sp)*, tr in same sp, ch 3, [(tr, ch 3, tr) in sp between next 2 picots, ch 3] around, join in 4th ch of beg ch-7. Fasten off. *(48 tr, 48 ch sps)*

Rnd 14: Join frosty green with sc in first ch sp, (sc, ch 3, 2 sc) in same sp, (2 sc, ch 3, 2 sc) in each ch sp around, join in beg sc. *(192 sc, 48 ch sps)*

Rnd 15: Sl st in next st, sl st in next ch sp, beg cl in same sp, ch 4, [cl in next ch sp, ch 4] around, join in beg cl. *(48 cls)*

Rnd 16: Ch 1, (sc, 3 dc, sc) in each ch sp around, join in beg sc. Fasten off. *(48 3-dc groups)*

Rnd 17: Join ecru with sc in **back lp** *(see Stitch Guide)* of center dc of any 3-dc group, working behind sts, 3 dc in top of next cl on rnd 15, [sc in back lp of center dc of next 3-dc group on last rnd, working behind sts, 3 dc in top of next cl on rnd 15] around, join in beg sc. Fasten off.

BORDER
3-TIERED ROSE
Rnd 1: With light pink, ch 6, join in beg ch to form ring, ch 1, 18 sc in ring, join in beg sc. *(18 sc)*

Rnd 2: Ch 1, sc in first st, ch 3, sk next 2 sts, [sc in next st, ch 3, sk next 2 sts] around, join in beg sc. *(6 sc, 6 ch sps)*

Rnd 3: For **petals**, ch 1, (sc, 5 dc, sc) in each ch sp around, join in beg sc. *(6 petals)*

Rnd 4: Working behind petals, ch 1, fpsc around post of first sc on rnd 2, ch 4, [fpsc around next sc on rnd 2, ch 4] around, join in beg sc. *(6 ch sps)*

Rnd 5: For **petals**, ch 1, (sc, 7 dc, sc) in each ch sp around, join in beg sc. *(6 petals)*

Rnd 6: Working behind petals, ch 1, fpsc around post of first sc on rnd 4, ch 5, [fpsc around next sc on rnd 4, ch 5] around, join in beg sc. *(6 ch sps)*

Rnd 7: For **petals**, ch 1, (sc, 9 dc, sc) in each of first 5 ch sps, (sc, 5 dc) in last ch sp, sl st in center st of any 3-dc group on last rnd of Doily, (4 dc, sc) in same ch sp on last rnd of Rose, join in beg sc. Fasten off. Mark center st of first Petal made.

[Sk next 7 3-dc groups on last rnd of Doily, work 3-Tiered Rose joining to next 3-dc group on Doily] 5 times for a total of 6 3-Tiered Roses.

2-TIERED ROSE
Rnd 1: With medium pink, ch 6, join in beg ch to form ring, ch 1, 18 sc in ring, join in beg sc. *(18 sc)*

Rnd 2: Ch 1, sc in first st, ch 3, sk next 2 sts, [sc in next st, ch 3, sk next 2 sts] around, join in beg sc. *(6 sc, 6 ch sps)*

Rnd 3: For **petals**, ch 1, (sc, 5 dc, sc) in each ch sp around, join in beg sc. *(6 petals)*

Rnd 4: Working behind petals, ch 1, fpsc around post of first sc on rnd 2, ch 4, [fpsc around next sc on rnd 2, ch 4 around, join in beg sc. *(6 ch sps)*

Rnd 5: For **petals**, ch 1, (sc, 7 dc, sc) in each of next 3 ch sps, (sc, 4 dc) in next ch sp, sl st in marked st on any 3-Tiered Rose, (3 dc, sc) in same ch sp on this Rose, (sc, 4 dc) in next ch sp, sk next 3-dc group on Doily, sl st in center st of next 3-dc group, (3 dc, sc) in same ch sp on this Rose, (sc, 4 dc) in next ch sp, sl st in center st of next 3-dc group on Doily, (3 dc, sc) in same ch sp on this Rose, join in beg sc. Fasten off.

Rep around Doily next to each 3-Tiered Rose.

6-POINT RING
With burgundy, ch 5, join in beg ch to form ring, ch 1, [2 sc in ring, ch 3, sl st in top of last st made] 3 times, 2 sc in ring, working on opposite side of 3-Tiered Rose, ch 1, sl st in 10th st on Doily from joining of 3-Tiered Rose, ch 1, 2 sc in ring, ch 3, sl st in top of last st made, 2 sc in ring, sl st in center st of next unworked petal after joining on 3-Tiered Rose, ch 1, join in beg sc. Fasten off.

Rep around Doily next to each 3-Tiered Rose.

12-POINT RING
With burgundy, ch 6, join in beg ch to form ring, ch 3 *(counts as first dc)*, dc in ring, ch 3, sl st in top of last st made, [2 dc in ring, ch 3, sl st in top of last st made] 8 times, 2 dc in ring, ch 1, sl st in center st of next unworked petal on 3-Tiered Rose after joining of 2-Tiered Rose,

ch 1, 2 dc in ring, ch 3, sl st in top of last st made, 2 dc in ring, ch 1, sl st in center st of next unworked petal on 2-Tiered Rose, ch 1, join in 3rd ch of beg ch-3. Fasten off.

Rep around Doily on each set of Roses.

LARGE LEAF

Note: Work rows in **back lps** *(see Stitch Guide) unless otherwise stated.*

Row 1: With frosty green, ch 11, sc in 2nd ch from hook and in each ch across, ch 3, working on opposite side of ch, sc in each next 7 chs, leaving rem chs unworked, turn. *(17 sc, 1 ch-3 sp)*

Row 2: Ch 2, sc in 2nd ch from hook, sc in each of next 7 sts, (sc, ch 3, sc) in next ch sp, sc in each of next 7 sts, leaving rem sts unworked, turn.

Rows 3–5: Ch 2, sc in 2nd ch from hook, sc in each of next 8 sts, (sc, ch 3, sc) in next ch sp, sc in each of next 7 sts, leaving rem sts unworked, turn. *(18 sc, 1 ch sp)*

Row 6: Ch 2, sc in 2nd ch from hook, sc in each of next 8 sts, (sc, ch 3, sc) in next ch sp, sc in each of next 7 sts, leaving rem sts unworked, ch 1, working on 1 6-Point Ring, sl st in first unworked ch-3 sp from joining on Doily, turn.

Row 7: Ch 1, sc in next ch, sc in each of next 8 sts, (sc, ch 3, sc) in next ch sp, sc in each of next 7 sts, leaving rem sts unworked, turn.

Row 8: Ch 2, sc in 2nd ch from hook, sc in each of next 8 sts, (sc, ch 3, sc) in next ch sp, sc in each of next 7 sts, leaving rem sts unworked, ch 1, sk next 3-dc group from joining on Doily, sl st in center st of next 3-dc group, turn.

Row 9: Ch 1, sc in next ch, sc in each of next 8 sts, sc in next ch sp, ch 1, sl st in sp between last joined petal and next unworked petal on 2-Tiered Rose, ch 1, sc in same ch sp on this Leaf, sc in each of next 7 sts, leaving rem sts unworked, turn.

Row 10: Ch 2, sc in 2nd ch from hook, sc in each of next 8 sts, sc in next ch sp, sl st in same sp between petals of 2-Tiered Rose as last joining, leaving rem sts unworked. Fasten off.

Rep Large Leaf around Doily in each sp between 6-Point Ring and 2-Tiered Rose.

SMALL LEAF

Note: Work rows in back lps unless otherwise stated.

Row 1: With frosty green, ch 7, sc in 2nd ch from hook and in each ch across, ch 3, working on opposite side of ch, sc in each of next 3 chs, leaving rem sts unworked, turn. *(9 sc, 1 ch sp)*

Row 2: Ch 2, sc in 2nd ch from hook, sc in each of next 3 chs, (sc, ch 3, sc) in next ch sp, sc in each of next 3 sts, leaving rem sts unworked, turn.

Rows 3 & 4: Ch 2, sc in 2nd ch from hook, sc in each of next 4 sts, (sc, ch 3, sc) in next ch sp, sc in each of next 3 sts, leaving rem sts unworked, turn. *(10 sc)*

Row 5: Ch 2, sc in 2nd ch from hook, sc in each of next 4 sts, (sc, ch 3, sc) in next ch sp, sc in each of next 3 sts, leaving rem sts unworked, ch 1, sl st in end of last row on Large Leaf, turn.

Row 6: Ch 1, sc in next ch, sc in each of next 4 sts, sc in next ch sp, ch 1, sl st in sp between next 2 unworked petals on 2-Tiered Rose, ch 1, sc in same sp on this Leaf, sc in each of next 3 sts, leaving rem sts unworked, turn.

Row 7: Ch 2, sc in 2nd ch from hook, sc in each of next 4 sts, sc in next ch sp, sl st in same sp between petals of 2-Tiered Rose as last joining, leaving rem sts unworked. Fasten off.

Rep Small Leaf around Doily on rem Large Leaves and 2-Tiered Roses. ∎

Rose Song

SKILL LEVEL

INTERMEDIATE

FINISHED SIZE

18 inches across

MATERIALS

- Size 10 crochet cotton:
  100 yds each burgundy and medium pink
  75 yds light pink
  50 yds each white and frosty green
- Size 7/1.65mm steel crochet hook or size needed to obtain gauge

GAUGE

Center Rose = 2¼ inches across

PATTERN NOTES

Join with a slip stitch unless otherwise stated.

Chain-5 at beginning of rounds counts as first double crochet and chain-2 space unless otherwise stated.

Chain-3 at beginning of rounds counts as first double crochet unless otherwise stated.

SPECIAL STITCHES

Picot: Ch 4, sl st in top of last st made.

Shell: (2 dc, ch 2, 2 dc) in designated place.

Triple picot: (Ch 4, sl st, ch 5, sl st, ch 4, sl st) in **front lp** (*see Stitch Guide*) of last st made.

INSTRUCTIONS

CENTER ROSE

Rnd 1: With burgundy, ch 5, **join** (*see Pattern Notes*) in beg ch, ch 1, 12 sc in ring, join in beg sc. (*12 sc*)

Rnd 2: Ch 1, sc in first st, ch 3, sk next st, [sc in next st, ch 3, sk next st] around, join in beg sc. (*6 sc, 6 ch sps*)

Rnd 3: For **petals**, ch 1, (sc, 5 dc, sc) in each ch sp around, join in beg sc. (*6 petals*)

Rnd 4: Sl st in next dc, ch 1, sc in same st, [ch 2, sc in next dc] 4 times, *sk next sc, sl st in sc on rnd 2, sk next sc on next petal, sc in first dc, [ch 2, sc in next dc] 4 times, rep from * around, join in joining sl st of last rnd. (*30 sc, 24 ch-2 sps*)

Rnd 5: Working behind petals, ch 1, **fpsc** (*see Stitch Guide*) around post of first sc on rnd 2, ch 4, [fpsc around next sc on rnd 2, ch 4 around, join in beg sc. (*6 ch sps*)

Rnd 6: For **petals**, ch 1, (sc, 7 dc, sc) in each ch sp around, join in beg sc. (*6 petals*)

Rnd 7: Sl st in next dc, ch 1, sc in same st, [ch 2, sc in next dc] 6 times, *sk next sc, sl st in sc on rnd 5, sk next sc on next petal, sc in first dc, [ch 2, sc in next dc] 6 times, rep from * around, join in joining sl st of last rnd. (*42 sc, 36 ch-2 sps*)

Rnd 8: Working behind petals, ch 1, fpsc around post of first sc on rnd 5, ch 5, [fpsc around next sc on rnd 5, ch 5] around, join in beg sc. (*6 ch sps*)

Rnd 9: For **petals**, ch 1, (sc, 9 dc, sc) in each ch sp around, join in beg sc. (*6 petals*)

Rnd 10: Sl st in next dc, ch 1, sc in same st, [ch 2, sc in next dc] 8 times, *sk next sc, sl st in sc on rnd 8, sk next sc on next petal, sc in first dc, [ch 2, sc in next dc] 8 times, rep from * around, join in joining sl st of last rnd. (*54 sc, 48 ch-2 sps*)

Rnd 11: Working behind petals, ch 1, fpsc around post of first sc on rnd 8, ch 6, [fpsc around next sc on rnd 8, ch 6] around, join in beg sc. (*6 ch sps*)

Rnd 12: For **petals**, ch 1, (sc, 12 dc, sc) in each ch sp around, join in beg sc. (*6 petals*)

Rnd 13: Sl st in next dc, ch 1, sc in same st, [ch 2, sc in next dc] 11 times, *sk next sc, sl st in sc on rnd 11, sk next sc on next petal, sc in first dc, [ch 2, sc in next dc] 11 times, rep from * around, join in joining sl st of last rnd. Fasten off.

FIRST LARGE ROSE

Rnds 1–8: With medium pink, rep rnds 1–8 of Center Rose.

Rnd 9: For **petals**, ch 1, (sc, 10 dc, sc) in each ch sp around, join in beg sc. *(6 petals)*

Rnd 10: Sl st in next dc, ch 1, sc in same st, [ch 2, sc in next dc] 9 times, *sk next sc, sl st in next sc on rnd 8, sk next sc on next petal, sc in next dc, [ch 2, sc in next dc] 9 times, rep from * 3 times, sk next sc, sl st in next sc on rnd 8, sk next sc on next petal, sc in next dc, [ch 2, sc in next dc] 4 times, ch 1, sl st in 6th ch sp of any petal on last rnd of Center Rose, ch 1, sc in next dc on this Rose, [ch 2, sc in next dc] 4 times, join in joining sl st of last rnd. Fasten off.

NEXT LARGE ROSE

Rnds 1–8: With medium pink, rep rnds 1–8 of Center Rose.

Rnd 9: For **petals**, ch 1, (sc, 10 dc, sc) in each ch sp around, join in beg sc. *(6 petals)*

Rnd 10: Sl st in next dc, ch 1, sc in same st, [ch 2, sc in next dc] 9 times, *sk next sc, sl st in next sc on rnd 8, sk next sc on next petal, sc in next dc, [ch 2, sc in next dc] 9 times, rep from * twice, sk next sc, sl st in next sc on rnd 8, sk next sc on next petal, sc in next dc, [ch 2, sc in next dc] 4 times, ch 1, sl st in center ch sp of first petal after joined petal on last Large Rose, ch 1, sc in next dc on this Rose, [ch 2, sc in next dc] 4 times, sk next sc, sl st in next sc on rnd 8, sk next sc on next petal, sc in next dc, [ch 2, sc in next dc] 4 times, ch 1, sl st in 6th ch sp of next petal on last rnd of Center Rose, ch 1, sc in next dc on this Rose, [ch 2, sc in next dc] 4 times, join in joining sl st of last rnd. Fasten off.

Rep Next Large Rose 3 times.

LAST LARGE ROSE

Rnds 1–8: With medium pink, rep rnds 1–8 of Center Rose.

Rnd 9: For **petals**, ch 1, (sc, 10 dc, sc) in each ch sp around, join in beg sc. *(6 petals)*

Rnd 10: Sl st in next dc, ch 1, sc in same st, [ch 2, sc in next dc] 9 times, *sk next sc, sl st in next sc on rnd 8, sk next sc on next petal, sc in next dc, [ch 2, sc in next dc] 9 times, rep from *, sk next sc, sl st in next sc on rnd 8, sk next sc on next petal, sc in next dc, [ch 2, sc in next dc] 4 times, ch 1, sl st in center ch sp of first petal after joined petal on last Large Rose, ch 1, sc in next dc on this Rose, [ch 2, sc in next dc] 4 times, sk next sc, sl st in next sc on rnd 8, sk next sc on next petal, sc in next dc, [ch 2, sc in next dc] 4 times, ch 1, sl st in 6th ch sp of next petal on last rnd of Center Rose, ch 1, sc in next dc on this Rose, [ch 2, sc in next dc] 4 times, sk next sc, sl st in next sc on rnd 8, sk next sc on next petal, sc in next dc, [ch 2, sc in next dc] 4 times ch 1, sl st in center ch sp of corresponding petal on first Large Rose, ch 1, sc in next dc on this Rose, [ch 2, sc in next dc] 4 times, join in joining sl st of last rnd. Fasten off.

MEDIUM ROSE

Rnds 1–5: With light pink, rep rnds 1–5 of Center Rose.

Rnd 6: For **petals**, ch 1, (sc, 8 dc, sc) in each ch sp around, join in beg sc. *(6 petals)*

Rnd 7: Sl st in next dc, ch 1, sc in same st, [ch 2, sc in next dc] 7 times, *sk next sc, sl st in sc on rnd 5, sk next sc on next petal, sc in first dc, [ch 2, sc in next dc] 7 times, rep from * 3 times, sk next sc, sl st in sc on rnd 5, sk next sc on next petal, sc in first dc, [ch 2, sc in next dc] 3 times, ch 1, sl st in center ch sp on center unworked petal of 1 Large Rose, ch 1, sc in next dc on this Rose, [ch 2, sc in next dc] 3 times, join in joining sl st of last rnd.

Rep Medium Rose 5 times, joining 1 to each Large Rose.

SMALL ROSE

Rnd 1: With white, ch 5, join in beg ch, ch 1, 12 sc in ring, join in beg sc. *(12 sc)*

Rnd 2: Ch 1, sc in first st, ch 3, sk next st, [sc in next st, ch 3, sk next st] around, join in beg sc. *(6 sc, 6 ch sps)*

Rnd 3: For **petals**, ch 1, (sc, 6 dc, sc) in each ch sp around, join in beg sc. *(6 petals)*

Rnd 4: Sl st in next dc, ch 1, sc in same st, [ch 2, sc in next dc] 5 times, *sk next sc, sl st in sc on rnd 2, sk next sc on next petal, sc in first dc, [ch 2, sc in next dc] 5 times, rep from * 3 times, sk next sc, sl st in sc on rnd 2, sk next sc on next petal, sc in first dc, [ch 2, sc in next dc] twice, ch 1, sk st in center ch sp of 3rd petal after joined petal on 1 Medium Rose, ch 1, sc in next dc on this Rose, [ch 2, sc in next dc] twice, join in joining sl st of last rnd. Fasten off.

Rep Small Rose 5 times, joining 1 to each Medium Rose.

DOILY

Rnd 1: Join frosty green in center ch sp of 3rd petal after joined petal of any Small Rose, **ch 5** *(see Pattern Notes)*, dc in same sp, *ch 7, (dc, ch 2, dc) in center ch sp of next petal, ch 6, (dc, ch 2, dc) in center ch sp of next petal, ch 7, (dc, ch 2, dc) in center ch sp of next unworked petal on next Medium Rose, ch 6, (dc, ch 2, dc) in center ch sp of next petal, ch 7, **tr dec** *(see Stitch Guide)* in center ch sps of next 2 unworked petals on Large Roses, **picot** *(see Special Stitches)*, ch 7, (dc, ch 2, sc) in center ch sp of next unworked petal on next Medium Rose, ch 6, (dc, ch 2, dc) in center ch sp of next petal, ch 7, (dc, ch 2, dc) in center ch sp of next unworked petal on next Small Rose, ch 6, (dc, ch 2, dc) in center ch sp of next petal, ch 7**, (dc, ch 2, dc) in center ch sp of next petal, rep from * around, ending last rep at **, join in 3rd ch of beg ch-5. *(54 2-dc groups, 54 ch-2 sps, 36 ch-7 sps, 24 ch-6 sps)*

Rnd 2: Sl st in next ch-2 sp, ch 5, dc in same sp, *[ch 2, (dc, ch 2) 3 times in next ch-7 sp, (dc, ch 2, dc) in next ch-2 sp, ch 2, (dc, ch 2) twice in next ch-6 sp, (dc, ch 2, dc) in next ch-2 sp] twice, [ch 3, dc in next ch-7 sp] twice, ch 3, [(dc, ch 2, dc) in next ch-2 sp, ch 2, (dc, ch 2) twice in next ch-6 sp, (dc, ch 2, dc) in next ch-2 sp, ch 2, (dc, ch 2) 3 times in next ch-7 sp] twice**, (dc, ch 2, dc) in next ch-2 sp, rep from * around, ending last rep at **, join in 3rd ch of beg ch-5. Fasten off. *(240 dc, 240 ch sps)*

Rnd 3: Join white in first ch-2 sp, ch 5, dc in same sp, *[ch 4, sk next ch sp, sc in next ch sp, ch 3, sc in next ch sp, ch 4, sk next ch sp, (dc, ch 2, dc) in next ch sp, ch 4, sk next ch sp, sc in next ch sp, ch 4, sk next ch sp, (dc, ch 2, dc) in next ch sp] twice, sk next ch sp, (dc, ch 4, sl st in 4th ch from hook, ch 1, dc) in next ch-3 sp, sk next ch sp, [(dc, ch 2, dc) in next ch sp, ch 4, sk next ch sp, sc in next ch sp, ch 4, sk next ch sp, (dc, ch 2, dc) in next ch sp, ch 4, sk next ch sp, sc in next ch sp, ch 3, sc in next ch sp, ch 4, sk next ch sp] twice**, (dc, ch 2, dc) in next ch sp, rep from * around, ending last rep at **, join in 3rd ch of beg ch-5. Fasten off. *(120 dc, 96 ch-4 sps, 72 sc, 60 ch-2 sps, 24 ch-3 sps)*

Rnd 4: Join light pink in first ch sp, **ch 3** *(see Pattern Notes)*, (dc, ch 2, 2 dc) in same sp, *ch 12, **shell** *(see Special Stitches)* in next ch-2 sp, [ch 9, shell in next ch-2 sp] twice, ch 9, sk next 2 ch-2 sps, shell in next ch-2 sp, [ch 9, shell in next ch-2 sp] twice, ch 12**, shell in next ch-2 sp, rep from * around, ending last rep at **, join in 3rd ch of beg ch-3. *(42 shells, 30 ch-9 sps, 12 ch-12 sps)*

Rnd 5: Join medium pink in first ch sp, ch 3, (dc, ch 2, 2 dc) in same sp, *ch 13, shell in ch sp of next shell, ch 9, shell in ch sp of next shell, ch 9, (2 dc, ch 3, sl st in top of last st made, 2 dc) in ch sp of next shell, shell in next ch-9 sp, (2 dc, ch 3, sl st in top of last st made, 2 dc) in ch sp of next shell, [ch 9, shell in ch sp of next shell] twice, ch 13**, shell in ch sp of next shell, rep from * around, ending last rep at **, join in 3rd ch of beg ch-3. Fasten off. *(36 shells, 24 ch-9 sps, 12 ch-13 sps)*

Rnd 6: Join burgundy in first ch sp, ch 3, (2 dc, ch 3, 3 dc) in same sp, *ch 6, sc around next ch sps of last 2 rnds at same time, ch 6, (3 dc, ch 3, 3 dc) in next shell, ch 4, sc around next ch sps of last 2 rnds at same time, ch 4, (3 dc, ch 3, 3 dc) in next shell, ch 4, sc around next ch sps of last 2 rnds at same time, ch 3, (3 dtr, ch 7, sl st in 6th ch from hook, ch 1, 3 dtr) in next shell, ch 3, sc around next ch sps of last 2 rnds at same time, ch 4, (3 dc, ch 3, 3 dc) in next shell, ch 4, sc around next ch sps of last 2 rnds at same time, ch 4, (3 dc, ch 3, 3 dc) in next shell, ch 6, sc around next ch sps of last 2 rnds at same time, ch 6**, (3 dc, ch 3, 3 dc) in next shell, rep from * around, ending last rep at **, join in 3rd ch of beg ch-3. *(180 dc, 42 ch-3 sps, 36 sc, 36 dtr, 36 ch-4 sps, 24 ch-6 sps, 6 ch-5 sps)*

Rnd 7: Ch 1, sc in each of first 3 sts, *(2 sc, **triple picot**—see Special Stitches, sc) in next ch sp, sc in each of next 3 sts, (3 sc, {ch 3, 3 sc} twice) in each of next 2 ch-6 sps, sc in each of next 3 sts, (2 sc, triple picot, sc) in next ch sp, sc in each of next 3 sts, (3 sc, ch 3, 3 sc) in each of 2 ch-4 sps, sc in each of next 3 sts, (2 sc, triple picot, sc) in next ch sp, sc in each of next 3 sts, (3 sc, ch 3, 3 sc) in next ch-4 sp, (2 sc, ch 3, 2 sc) in next ch-3 sp, sc in each of next 3 dtr, sc in next ch-1 sp, (2 sc, ch 3, 2 sc, triple picot, 2 sc, ch 3, 2 sc) in next ch-7 sp, sc in next ch-1 sp, sc in each of next 3 dtr, (2 sc, ch 3, 2 sc) in next ch-3 sp, (3 sc, ch 3, 3 sc) in next ch-4 sp, sc in each of next 3 sts, (2 sc, triple picot, sc) in next ch sp, sc in each of next 3 sts, (3 sc, ch 3, 3 sc) in each of next 2 ch-4 sps, sc in each of next 3 sts, (2 sc, triple picot, sc) in next ch sp, sc in each of next 3 sts, (3 sc, {ch 3, 3 sc} twice) in each of next 2 ch-6 sps**, sc in each of next 3 sts, rep from * around, ending last rep at **, join in beg sc. Fasten off. ∎

Stitch Guide

For more complete information, visit **FreePatterns.com**

ABBREVIATIONS

beg	begin/begins/beginning
bpdc	back post double crochet
bpsc	back post single crochet
bptr	back post treble crochet
CC	contrasting color
ch(s)	chain(s)
ch-	refers to chain or space previously made (i.e. ch-1 space)
ch sp(s)	chain space(s)
cl(s)	cluster(s)
cm	centimeter(s)
dc	double crochet (singular/plural)
dc dec	double crochet 2 or more stitches together, as indicated
dec	decrease/decreases/decreasing
dtr	double treble crochet
ext	extended
fpdc	front post double crochet
fpsc	front post single crochet
fptr	front post treble crochet
g	gram(s)
hdc	half double crochet
hdc dec	half double crochet 2 or more stitches together, as indicated
inc	increase/increases/increasing
lp(s)	loop(s)
MC	main color
mm	millimeter(s)
oz	ounce(s)
pc	popcorn(s)
rem	remain/remains/remaining
rep(s)	repeat(s)
rnd(s)	round(s)
RS	right side
sc	single crochet (singular/plural)
sc dec	single crochet 2 or more stitches together, as indicated
sk	skip/skipped/skipping
sl st(s)	slip stitch(es)
sp(s)	space(s)/spaced
st(s)	stitch(es)
tog	together
tr	treble crochet
trtr	triple treble
WS	wrong side
yd(s)	yard(s)
yo	yarn over

Chain—ch: Yo, pull through lp on hook.

Slip stitch—sl st: Insert hook in st, pull through both lps on hook.

Single crochet—sc: Insert hook in st, yo, pull through st, yo, pull through both lps on hook.

Front post stitch—fp: Back post stitch—bp: When working post st, insert hook from right to left around post st on previous row.

Back Front

Post of Stitch

Front loop—front lp Back loop— back lp

Front Loop   Back Loop

Half double crochet—hdc: Yo, insert hook in st, yo, pull through st, yo, pull through all 3 lps on hook.

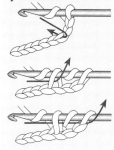

Double crochet—dc: Yo, insert hook in st, yo, pull through st, [yo, pull through 2 lps] twice.

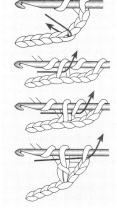

Change colors: Drop first color; with 2nd color, pull through last 2 lps of st.

Treble crochet—tr: Yo twice, insert hook in st, yo, pull through st, [yo, pull through 2 lps] 3 times.

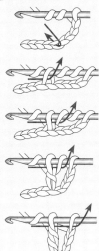

Double treble crochet—dtr: Yo 3 times, insert hook in st, yo, pull through st, [yo, pull through 2 lps] 4 times.

Single crochet decrease (sc dec): (Insert hook, yo, draw lp through) in each of the sts indicated, yo, draw through all lps on hook.

Example of 2-sc dec

Half double crochet decrease (hdc dec): (Yo, insert hook, yo, draw lp through) in each of the sts indicated, yo, draw through all lps on hook.

Example of 2-hdc dec

Double crochet decrease (dc dec): (Yo, insert hook, yo, draw loop through, draw through 2 lps on hook) in each of the sts indicated, yo, draw through all lps on hook.

Example of 2-dc dec

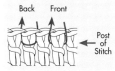

Example of 2-tr dec

Treble crochet decrease (tr dec): Holding back last lp of each st, tr in each of the sts indicated, yo, pull through all lps on hook.

US		UK
sl st (slip stitch)	=	sc (single crochet)
sc (single crochet)	=	dc (double crochet)
hdc (half double crochet)	=	htr (half treble crochet)
dc (double crochet)	=	tr (treble crochet)
tr (treble crochet)	=	dtr (double treble crochet)
dtr (double treble crochet)	=	ttr (triple treble crochet)
skip	=	miss

TOLL-FREE ORDER LINE or to request a free catalog (800) LV-ANNIE (800) 582-6643
Customer Service (800) AT-ANNIE (800) 282-6643, **Fax** (800) 882-6643
Visit anniesattic.com

We have made every effort to ensure the accuracy and completeness of these instructions.
We cannot, however, be responsible for human error, typographical mistakes or variations in individual work.

ISBN: 978-1-59635-216-2

Printed in USA

2 3 4 5 6 7 8 9